To request permissions, contact the publisher at bczpublishers@gmail.com

Paperback: ISBN 978-1-7367153-8-3

First Paperback Edition: December 2022

Written by: Mina Soliman
Illustrated by: Cynthia Zeilenga

BCZ Publishers
3365 E Miraloma Ave Ste 205, Anaheim, CA 92806

BCZ
PUBLISHERS

how i helped...

Moses Save God's People

"The Lord Himself will lead you and be with you. He will not fail you or abandon you, so do not lose courage or be afraid."
Deuteronomy 31:8

As a small seed I was carried into dirt
And when it rained, I spread my roots
But because of the harsh earth
I didn't know if I would ever bear fruits

Instead of a large and beautiful tree
I grew into a bush, small and thorny
I wished for a larger purpose in life
But for now, my wish could not be

I watched as the other trees
Were used to build a beautiful town
I tried to keep my faith strong
Even though I felt so down

I prayed to the Lord with every leaf and branch
For His love to fill my heart
How much longer could I stand
Before my branches begin to wither apart

I knew the Lord had a purpose for me
Ever since I was placed into the dirt
And through the power of His great love
Feelings of calm replaced all the hurt

One day, I heard footsteps along the path
Which brought a sense of joy to my ears
A man named Moses trailed forward with his staff
For him, I knew I had waited all these years

Moses wanted his people to live without pain
As many suffered being poor and ill
They'd lost faith in God's promise and plan
Being forced to carry out the Pharaoh's will

I was then consumed by fire, but it didn't burn me
As Moses fell to his knees, amazed
The Lord spoke of the need to free
The Israelites in the coming days

"And to those with faith that had all but given up"
Said a voice that could be heard in the sky
The God of Abraham, Isaac, and Jacob
Commanded that their spirits be lifted high

And though I could have been a house or boat
Or other creations, royal and grand
The Lord had a different purpose for me
To help lead His people towards the Promised Land

The End.

PUBLISHERS